D1457303

LOVING YOURSELF ISN'T SELFISH

By Chelle Shapiro

How to Stop
Internalizing
Emotions &
Persevere
Against All Odds

Book Cover & Logo Design: Chelle Shapiro

Book Coach: Linda Vettrus-Nichols
www.LindaVettrus-Nichols.com

Dedication

"This book is dedicated to me,
because for once in my fucking life,
I've finally chosen me."

Contents

Acknowledgments

My deepest gratitude to Linda Vettrus-Nichols and Terry Earthwind Nichols for encouraging me to walk at the level of my soul and speak my truths.

My utmost appreciation to Jennifer Beitz for challenging me to shatter my limiting beliefs.

To my dear friend, Wendy Gilhula: Thank you for reawakening my creative spirit.

From the bottom of my heart, thank you to my family.

Thank you to my mom for urging me to reach out, stay in touch, connect with others, and put myself out there.

Thank you to my dad for instilling courage in me to stand by my decisions no matter the outcome.

Thank you to my brother and sister, who have always supported me and held space for me to be myself.

...And to the rest of those who inspired the teachings in this book and will not read it, I love you and I forgive you. Had it not been for you, I would not be who I am, where I am, and doing what I love today.

Chapter 1

Internalizing Emotions

I come from a very loving family, so I didn't really come from a place of feeling unloved and unwanted. What happened throughout my childhood and on into adulthood was that I was silenced a lot. I was told that I couldn't speak up. I was told that I needed to contain my emotions and to reign them in so other people couldn't see them. Until a few years ago, I thought that this was the norm.

I began to realize it didn't just happen with my parents. It also happened with teachers at school. They evidently thought that I was always raising my hand because I needed to prove myself. All I wanted to do was spark a conversation. I wanted to ask questions... not just put my hand up and be like... 'I know the answer!'

One of my first teenage experiences of being silent and feeling powerless happened during the summer after my freshman year in high school. I worked as a lifeguard at a private pool down the block from my home. Most days I arrived early. I enjoyed the quiet time by the pool before the chaos of the day.

I arrived one morning, and no one came out of the office to say hello. I could hear noise, so I took the initiative to let the staff know I had arrived for my shift. I called out several times to ask who was there. When I didn't get a response, I knocked on the counter and said, "I'm here for my shift, I just wanted to say good morning." No response. I walked around the counter and could see that one of the office doors was open. I called out good morning, and as I passed by, I saw my boss sitting in the dark with porn on the screen. I didn't stick around to get a closer look. I didn't even know what I had seen. I do know I had startled him, and I'm pretty sure he saw me.

I headed straight for the pool. When another lifeguard arrived a few minutes later I told her what had happened. For some reason I felt like I had done something wrong. It was my fault. I looked into a dark room. I should have knocked louder. I shouldn't have gone to work early. The news spread like wildfire.

Lifeguards and other staff members kept coming up to me and asking me what had happened. It was like playing telephone, because the story they thought they had heard kept changing. I remember feeling tense all day. There was a huge 'knot like' feeling in my throat. I was afraid to speak. Without any doubt I knew I couldn't talk about it again.

So not being allowed or able to speak my truth came from all different areas of my life. The stress and anxiety built up to the point where I was eventually afraid to speak up at all.

I was especially afraid to say the wrong thing. I was also so afraid to upset people that I started to internalize all of my emotions and that's when things became really toxic.

I kept myself secluded in my own bubble and felt like I couldn't share. Within this past year I told myself 'screw everybody else, I need to speak, there's a reason that I have a voice, and I want to use it!'

This past year has really been about transformation... with me unleashing my voice and leaving a job after 13 years.

Chapter 2

Against All Odds

When I graduated from college, it took me awhile to find a job. Even though I graduated as a graphic designer, I'm a creative, so I don't think of myself as just a graphic designer.

When I finally had my first job interview, I went to that interview with this huge portfolio. I didn't know what to expect. The person interviewing me only looked at two or three things. Then said, "Okay, we have this project right now and I don't have anybody to work on it. Would you like to see if you can handle it?

I agreed and was immediately put to work at a really old and very slow computer. I almost laughed out loud. The computer kept crashing and I had to restart a few times. It kept losing things that it hadn't saved before it crashed, even though it was on autosave. A true red flag that they didn't have their systems up to date.

Later I realized they didn't have any systems in place to really allow me to do my job to the best of my ability. I knocked that project out and it took me all day to do it. I stuck with it and got it done.

After that first day, I felt really pleased with myself... like, 'hey, I didn't give up'. I showed them that I could do it. I had all these challenges and setbacks and I still got through it. I felt really good about that at the end of the day. If they had been testing me to see how I reacted, what they got out of it was 'we put her in this horrible situation, gave her all of these obstacles, and she took it'. I think about that sometimes. I'm like, did they actually know that's what they were doing? Did they have that intention in the first place?

Looking back, I sometimes wonder, 'how did they see it?' I'll never know the answer to that question and that's okay.

What started happening over time was that I would finish the work I had been given, and instead of just sitting there waiting for them to bring me something else, I would ask my boss or coworkers for more.

What do you have? What can I help with?

I kept thinking that I was somehow earning their trust. I was showing them that I could be a little bit more versatile than just a graphic designer and they could throw me in wherever they needed me. That's exactly what started to happen. They heard me and they kept piling it on until it wasn't manageable for me anymore. I kept going and it became overwhelming.

Even now, I live by myself and I'm very independent. I like to do things for me. I'm also very introverted so I don't necessarily have this need to go out at night. I'm the type of person who can easily go straight home from work to relax and unwind from the day. If I needed to stay late at work to get things done, that wasn't a big deal for me.

However, there was never any 'thank you so much Chelle', we really appreciate it. We know you're probably exhausted. Why don't you come in a little later tomorrow; just take your time in the morning and get some rest. There was none of the sort.

Everything built up, one thing on top of another, day after day. There really was no end in sight. It was like how long can I keep banging my head against the wall?

As I look back, I was people pleasing the whole time I was with that company. It really took its toll on me. I was stressed out, worried, and having panic attacks. My mind was constantly in 'what did I forget to do, and who did I forget to help' mode. At that point my people pleasing mentality had become detrimental to my health and wellbeing. It was affecting my ability to get things done well, and to help other people.

More to the point, my boss and coworkers could see I was breaking down and yet that didn't stop them from adding more things to my plate. I was naturally good at doing things and getting things done. The attitude was, 'Oh well she'll just stick it out, she'll survive. She'll get it done anyway. We don't even need to give this a second thought or worry about her at all. She'll stay no matter what she's going through.'

So, they acknowledged what was going on and yet weren't about to do anything about it. They just kept things the way they were. That's where the toxicity part came into the picture.

My boss and coworkers saw me break down on multiple occasions. For instance, having a nervous breakdown bawling my eyes out in fetal position on the floor or having a panic attack.

I didn't feel like I had any support.

At one point I even asked if they could define my role a little bit more. What exactly did I need to do and what could somebody else do? I also wanted to know if they could take some of the responsibilities off my plate. The only response I got was no.

I never really took vacations for myself, and even when I took a day off, I was still working. I could never seem to really separate myself from my job.

I was burnt out and sick, both physically and mentally. I didn't have any boundaries in place or know what they even looked like. I didn't stand up for myself, take care of myself or do anything to get me out of those situations. I was also still very much in need of healing for myself. I knew that staying at this job wasn't the right thing for me. It was a very toxic environment, and I wasn't going anywhere but down.

At one point I asked for a meeting with my boss; by the end of the meeting, I was like... Wait. What? You just agreed to have a conversation with me about how I could scale back so that we could be more productive, feel better, and make strategic moves as a company. If you want me to help you grow, you also get to let me grow. This whole conversation with me was to be about boundaries and priorities. I wanted to know what things would look like for me going forward. All you can say is just keep doing 'everything'?

That was a definitive moment for me, knowing I was doing the right thing by giving them my notice to leave.

Before I gave my notice to quit, I didn't tell anybody about that idea. I decided to take two weeks of vacation time. I put it on the company's calendar so they couldn't say that I didn't do it properly.

Even though I knew I'd be leaving, I wanted to take this time to separate myself and to also see if I could slow down. I wondered if I'd even be the slightest bit better after two weeks. I called it Operation Separation. I also determined that it didn't matter what anybody said when they found out I was going to quit my job, even though I didn't have a plan for my future yet.

Chapter 3

Operation Separation

The first week was so hard. I was answering emails left and right, because I didn't want to disappoint people. The next week I was able to relax a little bit. I stopped checking my email a million times a day. I limited myself to 2 or 3 times a day, I even set a timer. Just that slight adjustment was life changing, it was like a rush and I was like 'oh my god, this is what freedom feels like?' I was hooked.

I did go back to work after the 2 weeks were up. Even though I had already given my notice, I stuck around for about a month. I wanted to transition smoothly.

Tying up loose ends became an almost impossible task when my boss hired my replacement and wanted me to train him. I couldn't understand why someone else couldn't train him and show him around. On the first day my replacement came to work, I was instructed to sit with him in my office and guide him through the day-to-day operations, show him the ropes, and how to do things. However, all he wanted to do was hit on me. GREAT! Should I just chalk that up too? It had happened many times before. As one of the only women within the company ranks, it actually happened often.

How many times had I been made to feel uncomfortable at work? The unwelcomed eyeballs looking everywhere except in my eyes. Unwanted advances and an arm reaching across me and just happening to graze my breasts.

I'll never forget the time a coworker exposed himself to me and got little more than a pat on the back. Wink, wink, nod, nod. How many times had I reported it to my boss, only to be told to let it slide? How many times had I been told that I must be overthinking it and there was no way so-and-so meant anything by it?

My fault, it was always my fault.

I must have asked for it. Now that I was headed out the door, I certainly didn't have to chalk it up and I knew that I no longer needed to feel like I had to.

I was leaving. I didn't need to stand for it or sit through any more of it. I moved myself out of my office to the opposite end of the production floor, so I didn't have to feel so uncomfortable. Unlike all the other times before, this time I went above my boss with my complaint. I went to his wife. I thought, maybe another woman could understand the severity of the situation. She reacted with disbelief, which only led to more humiliation for me. On Day 2 of training my replacement, I was summoned into my boss' office and persuaded not to file a formal complaint. I was also urged once again to suck it up and stay in my own office with my trainee. My boss' exact words were, "You have to stay put."

I didn't need to do anything! Not for him anyway and certainly not for my replacement. It was time to cut the cord and to separate myself once and for all.

Before leaving for good, my boss hit me with a particular game changing comment: "You'll never succeed without us." I also heard that from several other people because they were probably pissed that I was leaving. In other words, they'd have more work to do.

I never felt so alone.

At the end of the day, it was just me. No one was there for me. No one had my best interests in mind.

The greatest feeling after leaving that job was when my mother said, "That was a really courageous move you made. I wish I could do something similar. I wish I could have the guts to do that." My mother had never spoken like that to me before. It was really a supportive and affirming moment for me. It was also very eye opening that I actually needed that validation and it felt so good.

Chapter 4

You Don't Know
What You Don't Know

How many times in your life has someone asked you this question, "How come you didn't know that?" or said, "You should have known better." Since my transformation my response to those questions or comments is "Screw you!"

Let's get real. How could I have possibly known what was in someone else's head? If I'd never been exposed to something, how would I know about it? To know or even to have the slightest inkling what someone else wanted isn't on me, it's on them.

How can anyone expect us to know what we don't know? It makes you really question yourself like, why didn't I know that and why did I let them down? This is what happens when we let others 'project' their issues onto us. That's such a huge moment when you can quickly process 'it's not on me, that's on you for not communicating better'. This is a skill that is really important for people to learn. You're not expected to know everything right off the bat.

We also get to remember not to hold others accountable, just because we already know something they don't. We can't hold something against them for not knowing what they don't know.

We also don't always know how to pass something on to somebody else.

Working with someone else or hiring someone to work with you takes patience. There's a bit of an adjustment period that needs to take place. It takes time and good communication skills before you are truly understanding of each other.

If I hire somebody to do something for me, I'm hiring them for a reason. I hired them for their expertise. I can't possibly assess what they know. I hire people because I want them to tell me what to do or do it for me. I hire them because I'm seeking expert advice or skills.

Trip Wires in the Hiring Process

Even though I haven't hired any employees for my business, I do believe that the easiest way to go is to hire smarter. Also, to hire slowly and fire quickly. Having lots of trip wires in the hiring process makes sense to me. You can watch to see who stalls out, who jumps ahead and makes a decision without you. Who comes running back? That's all very interesting.

Trip Wires in the Connection Process

When it comes to connecting online, I tend to only connect

with people who have taken the time to send me messages. I can tell a great deal from those messages how interested they are in actually getting to know me vs. pitching me. If I get an automated message. Forget it!

Connecting with others has always felt like I had to put in extra effort. When I was a little girl I tended to run back to my mother and hold her hand if I was approached by anyone I didn't know. My mother is a very outgoing person. Wherever we went, she would strike up a conversation.

Chatting with others was like breathing for her. She encouraged me to meet new people. When I'd return home, she'd ask me questions like: Who did you meet today? Are you going to see them again? What did you talk about?

When it comes to networking for my business it's a different story. I enjoy meeting other entrepreneurs. I'm always curious as to why and how they started their business. I learn so much meeting people during a virtual call or in person.

Finding Your Tribe

When looking for your tribe it's important to network. You'll want to surround yourself with people who can help you succeed.

When I am passionate about something, I want to go all in... full steam ahead. When someone on LinkedIn reaches out to connect with me, the first thing I do is go to their profile and click on Mutual Connections to see who we both know. When I see who we have in common, I think about who those people are and how they have interacted with me. The next thing I do is skim through the potential connection's profile to see how serious they are about connecting. I also look to see if we have anything in common.

Chapter 5

Self-Care & Mental Health

As I mentioned earlier, I had become pretty sick and burnt out by the end of my 13-year tenure. That just didn't happen overnight. I could finish my work in a fraction of the time, that's the downside to being a high performing, overachieving, people pleaser. Instead of sitting idly, I wanted more. I asked for more. I wanted to show I could handle more responsibility. The more I asked the more I received, and as other employees left, I got tasked with their workloads too.

Pretty soon I was doing the work of at least 3 or 4 people. It became the norm to give me more and more work. You think I'm kidding? My boss told my coworkers to come to me for everything. I would make sure it all got done and done right. If they fell behind, it became my job to catch them up. Where's the teamwork in that? I was taking on their work, while they were taking the credit for getting it done. When my boss would speak to clients, he would often tell them that the team would do whatever they could to get the job done. The team he was talking about was me.

As a team of one, I didn't have a free moment. I only had like 30 seconds before somebody walked in again needing something from me. There were times I didn't eat at all because I was so busy doing all the things that I couldn't break free. I didn't take a few moments to replenish myself and refuel. That's a huge boundary issue. My thinking was 'everybody needs me to get things done'. There were no ifs ands or buts about it, I just needed to be on my game all of the time. I didn't have a free moment to myself all day long.

I eliminated self-care from my routine because in my mind, 'taking care of everyone else was more important than taking care of myself'. That was the result of me asking for more work and people bringing all those things to me. I put other people ahead of myself. That's the biggest boundary that I still struggle with every day. I am working on not having to stay so conscious about it. I'm working to create new neural pathways so that it's a subconscious automatic response to put my needs first. I am a people pleaser and I enjoy helping other people feel good. There's nothing wrong with that. As long as I don't forget my own needs in the process.

Failing Forward

When you're learning something new, you're gonna make a mistake, you're gonna make lots of mistakes. I fail forward on a daily basis. Mistakes are just learning experiences.

If I don't learn from my mistakes, that means I'm just gonna be doomed to keep repeating them. That's a huge hamster wheel I don't choose to run on. I always enjoy being better than the day, week, month or year before. So, if I can tweak one little thing to improve my experience and get better, I'm happy. Making a few mistakes before it's really drilled into my brain is fine with me. It's a process that we all need to go through.

I believe that if you're not failing forward, you're not going to be moving forward.

Imposter Syndrome

Am I good enough? Are people going to believe that I actually know what I'm doing? We can all get so caught up in our heads. It's like paralysis, you can't move forward. Sometimes you can't even figure out why.

So much of my life, my career, my success has been attached to my ability to help others and feel good about it. I beat myself up at the thought of letting others down.

I hold myself to an unattainable standard. I do it often. I keep myself stuck by blaming it on others. After all, I've been conditioned to be this way.

The thing is that's my own perception of myself. I project my own failure. Notice how I said 'project' and not predict. You get back tenfold what you put out into the world. Right? I don't predict the future, I manifest it. And when I only put negative energy out there and look for things to hold me back, of course that's all I will ever find. That's what I'm looking for.

If we're being completely honest, I'm doing it right now because in my own eyes, I'll never be good enough. That's terrifying.

Dancing around this same fear can go on forever. The fear isn't going away. Ultimately, I still need to do it. I still need to put myself out there. The sooner I get out of my comfort zone, and the more often I do it, the better. Great things never come from comfort zones, they come from taking a risk and doing it anyways. In other words, do it afraid.

Chapter 6

Fear

The fear of letting others down kept me stuck for way too long. I fed into the constant fear that 'others couldn't see how good I was'. I used to think that by learning all of the 'ins and outs' of the business, I could easily move up in the ranks and grow with the company. It took me a long time to realize that the company had other plans.

My growth wasn't one of them.

We can keep fear from holding us back, it just doesn't feel that way. Fear feels like a goddamn amusement park. You can tell yourself it's all fun and games but every ride and attraction, keeps your heart from just barely leaping out of your chest.

Take the merry-go-round - a glorified hamster wheel. You ride a magical-looking toy horse around in circles for a few minutes. It may look pretty, but you come off feeling dizzy from seeing the same things go by over and over again. Do you come off feeling merry at all?

The roller coaster, on the other hand is a thrill ride capturing all the fear and excitement of not knowing what twists and turns are coming next. You may temporarily boost your adrenalin by staring death in the face and defying gravity. When the excitement wears off, that queasiness in your stomach is enough to make you swear you'll never do it again.

And the bumper cars. You are literally driving a car with the sole intent to prevent others from getting by you, by jolting them back and vice versa. How's that for a jolt back to reality?

Fear is instilled in us from everywhere. It's used to wear us down for the very purpose of keeping us from moving forward. It teaches us to stay down and hold ourselves back.

So, what do we do with all of this bottled-up negative energy? We can channel it.

Let's take fear at face value; fear is an illusion. Just like the amusement park with all of the rides and attractions, fear gets your heart racing. Is it excitement? Actually, yes. What if you used that excitement to move yourself forward? Kind of like feel the fear and do it anyways, rather than looking at fear as a negative emotion.

Scarcity is a form of fear and shows up when we are out of alignment with ourselves.

Fear can show up as anxiety, insecurity, and within our dreams. Nightmares are not fun.

Fear comes from a lack of clarity. It's easy to go into procrastination mode when we aren't clear about what we want or who we want in our lives.

Fear is actually a positive sign that only comes around when you are doing something new or unfamiliar.

When it comes to fear, it's about being 'shakeable' like a tree. We can be with the fear and yet not let it snap us in half.

When you are afraid that you aren't doing enough in your business, TRUST YOUR HARD WORK. IT'S UNLOCKING DOORS YOU CAN'T SEE YET.

When it comes to relationships, remember that they take time to build. Unlike how it might have been meeting your bestie. You grabbed for the same donut and then boom, you're instant friends.

Professionally, it doesn't really work that way. You end up working to see who truly aligns with you. This takes more effort.

Does fear tend to hold you back?

Can you relate to any of these scenarios...

*You apply for a job, but you never actually get around to reaching out to the hiring manager because deep down you know someone else is probably a better fit. So why even try?

*You interviewed for your dream job....and you think it went well. But it's been a few days and you haven't heard anything from them. At the risk of sounding needy, you skip sending them a follow up note.

*You're feeling a bit salty that those new connections you made haven't panned out. You know you should probably reach out, but what's the use? They're not going to help you anyway. Right? Wrong!

If any of these sound like you... GIRRRRRL... we need to talk about building up your confidence.

STOP SELLING YOURSELF SHORT!

Chapter 7

Smartest Person in the Room

It's okay! You don't need to be the smartest person in the room. I don't feel like the smartest person in the room, and I have this inkling that other people think that I need to be.

That comes from years of experience doing the same things, learning, and knowing what's the best solution. I don't mind jumping in and asserting myself so that I keep somebody from making a horrible mistake. I'm always wanting to walk a person through the process they need to learn so they can do it for themselves. This way, it's not just me doing the thing for the sake of doing the thing.

I also don't treat things as a one and done, 'here's how you do it and now you should know what you are doing'. No one can ever learn from that type of teaching. As I already mentioned, I really feel like people always think that I need to be the smartest person in the room. I do want people to sometimes figure it out for themselves. I'm also happy to gently guide them through something that I already know.

What's wrong with not being the smartest person in the room?

Why would anybody want to be the smartest one?

How can you connect with others if you feel and exude that you're the smartest person?

You don't have to have all the answers.

There's the saying that if you're the smartest person in the room, get a new room. How are you supposed to have any kind of personal growth if you don't?

Outside of a work environment I'm never considered the smartest person in the room. I always surround myself with people I want to learn from. People who are seeking or are at a level where I am choosing to go.

If you want to reach new heights...

FIND SOMEONE WHO HAS ALREADY BEEN THERE.

They can show you the way.

And that, my friends, is why it's so important to build your network and nurture those relationships. If you don't know someone, someone in your circle does.

I ask myself questions like...

*Do I need to be in this room?

*Who else can I put in this room?

*That's how I roll.

I really enjoy being in a room full of people who know more than I do. That really nurtures my love for learning.

During my 13-year tenure I WAS the smartest person in the room and everybody else knew it. Without the pressure of having to do 'all the things', I would have loved training the staff for the sake of the company so we could have been a well-oiled machine. If I had to choose between learning and teaching others, I'd choose teaching.

Delegating without the support of my boss, made teaching impossible. Nobody wanted to learn. Everyone was quite happy having me carry the full load.

Chapter 8

Be Better Than Yesterday

That's always a nice challenge. It doesn't mean like be 1000 times better tomorrow than you were the day before or do all of the work. If you're hard on yourself, you can kind of stop and say, 'wait a minute, I wasn't able to do this yesterday or this didn't look as good or go as well yesterday as it did today'.

Every day is a new day to wake up and be great.

Some days I just don't want to join the party, and that's okay.

Some days I need to rest.

Those are what I call Me Days.

These are the days I allow myself to have that down time. This way I know that tomorrow I can start fresh with a clear mind and attack the day in a different way.

When I take time for myself, I don't stay stuck in whatever I was dealing with the day before. I grow more when I take time to relax and nurture my thoughts. I also use that time to encourage my body to replenish and repair itself. This way I can build on a strong foundation, learn faster, and move forward with ease.

We are never really stuck we can always shift into a new perspective. Mindset shifts are all about growth.

5 Tips to Avoid Feeling Stuck

1. Focus on the things that are within your control.

2. Stay in the present moment.

3. Acknowledge your feelings and figure out where they are coming from.

4. Allow your feelings to move through you.

5. Maintain a positive attitude.

My Biggest Champion

The most difficult challenge so far in having my own business has been changing my mindset and sticking with it. That's not to say I'm going to quit what I'm doing anytime soon. I'm doing important work and I'm not going to let anyone knock me off this path.

Naysayers are everywhere, old habits are still lurking in the shadows. It can be difficult not to slip. My passion and perseverance have kept me fighting and failing forward. I've learned to be my biggest champion throughout this journey.

Dreams & Reality

We've all grown up listening to the famous I HAVE A DREAM speech, by Dr. Martin Luther King Jr. How much time have any of us spent learning from his actions and the steps he took to empower others and make his dream come true?

Here's what I've figured out...

*It becomes very easy to blur the lines between dreams and reality.

*If you don't take the steps to make your dreams a reality, then they are just dreams.

*If you take action and work towards the intentional goals that you set for yourself, a dream will stop being unrealistic and become real.

*Dreams don't come true overnight.

*When you work to make your dreams come true, you leave a legacy that will continue to empower others to rise.

Martin Luther King Jr. took action to make sure his dreams would be realized. He wanted people to live in a world where they would feel safe, unjudged, and included for whoever they were... regardless of their background, gender, race, religion or any other bias. He may not have been a woman or identified as one, but he paved the way for women and men to speak more openly about diversity and inclusion.

So where did his dream end?

It didn't.

The difficult conversations he started have continued for generations. His dream and his actions have served, supported, and empowered others to close the gaps. That dream of his has helped me.

Now I'm not comparing myself to this hero, but I dream a lot and then I wake up. Actually, my dreams are often so vivid that I wake up feeling with my entire being that they were real. Even though I know my dreams aren't real, they enable me to see many possible outcomes. This empowers me to do things that I might not have done.

Chapter 9

Happiness Over Perfection

I'm definitely a recovering perfectionist. I used to attack something over and over again until I felt it was good enough. I eventually realized I'm never gonna be good enough and what I'm working on is never going to attain my version of perfect. So now, at one point I just stop and get it out there. My new mantra is "It's good enough and I'm good enough. In fact, I am enough."

When we obsess over being perfect and getting that immaculate version out there, more often than not, nobody else even notices.

The people who think that what we put out online is really good, whether we do or not, are most likely our people, our target audience so to speak. The people who don't like what we put out are not our people in the first place. They are not the right audience.

Allow yourself the happiness that comes from completing something, no matter how you feel about it, even if it's not perfect, especially if it's not perfect. Figure out how you will make it 1% better next time.

Perfect is Not the Answer

It's nice to be able to ask others for specific feedback or have an extra pair of eyes on what we are producing. People tend to feel needed when we ask for help. They might even point out something that we missed. That doesn't mean that it's not perfect or that it's not as close to perfect as it's going to be.

Feedback opens my eyes to think about something in a way that I maybe wouldn't have thought of on my own. It's like having frosting on our cake. I don't know about you, but I like both!

I also like to replace the word Perfect with Progress or Improvement. Perfect is not the solution. Progress is the solution. Improvement is the solution. To what? Stepping out of the fear of failure and the need to have everything perfect in your life before moving forward or releasing content into the world.

I used to acknowledge what could happen if I made a certain decision. That would get me planning various scenarios for all possible outcomes. I felt like I had to prepare for every single outcome. Now when I acknowledge the possible outcomes of a decision, I just remind myself that it won't be the end of the world if things don't work out or if I flub up.

Instead of thinking up all of the possible outcome scenarios, I can freely tell myself 'we'll cross that bridge when we come to it'. If and when we do get to it. I've had to restrain myself quite a bit from doing all that extra work that I probably didn't need to do in the first place.

Being In Our Heads

Being up in our heads causes a lot of anxiety. It causes a lot of overwhelm and it causes a lot of sleepless nights. It's what caused me to suffer from Imposter Syndrome and why I found myself on the floor at work bawling my eyes out. My anxiety definitely came about from me being in my head, questioning my every move.

This year has been difficult quitting my job WITHOUT a plan. Although, I felt the freedom of not having to plan things out every day.

It felt liberating. Until it didn't.

I was constantly hard on myself for not having a plan. I was figuring things out as I went through my new entrepreneurial journey. The anxiety came from not being able to see the finish line.

I tested the waters... A LOT. I pivoted. I niched down. I went with the flow.

The regimented, brainwashed planner in me was still making plans.

I've been realizing a lot lately that the mind still works even when the body takes a break.

Chapter 10

Reflect on the Past

In order to figure out how we got to where we are today, it's important to reflect on our past. I was shocked when I thought back to one of my favorite kid's songs. I had a VHS tape of various kid songs that taught kids how to do things and be in the world.

The title of the song is Bend Me Shape Me. For this particular song there were kids doing gymnastics on the video. The message was to be flexible in the world. However, the lyrics created a different story. For example, "Bend me shape me anyway you want me, as long as you love me, it's alright. Bend me, shape me, anyway you want me, you've got the power to turn on the light."

How wrong is that when you think about it? Someone else has the power to bend us and shape us? Holy shit!! This is the song that taught me it was okay for people to walk all over me. It's no wonder I felt powerless and gave my power away.

When I was 2 years old, my parents had just gotten a new camcorder. The type of video camera that had a VHS tape in it and when you were done filming, you put it in your VCR player and watched it on TV.

One day, my dad and I were sitting on a bench and my mom was filming. We were facing each other, and our legs were spread and hanging over the sides. I was having fun pouring change out of my little coin purse onto the bench. I daintily picked up each coin as I put them back into my purse. Then I'd shake it to hear the jingle.

At one point my dad scooped up the coins and held them in his hand. I said, "Hey those are mine, give them back." He held up a coin and said, "I'll give this one back, after you give me a kiss." After several 'no's' I caved in and gave him a kiss. It didn't stop there.

We continued this sick game until my purse was full.

I watched that video about 8 months ago. It was so shocking to see what had happened. My parents saw it as a game. That was NOT how I felt about it. Even though I didn't want to work for affection, I enjoyed the attention.

Playing catch was something I used to do on the front lawn with my dad. One day, when I was 12 years old, we were having a catch on the lawn. I remember he threw the softball and it hit me in the chest. It was the first time I ever had consciously thought about having boobs. I wasn't wearing a bra yet and there they were. The ball had hit me really hard the pain had hit me harder. Yep, I had boobs.

I remember crying and telling my dad that he had hurt me.

When I said, "Ouch, that really hurt!" He said, "Suck it up, it's not that bad. Let's keep playing." I remember running across the lawn and because of the lingering pain, becoming acutely aware that my breasts were bouncing. I had never really paid attention to that sensation before. I glanced at my dad as he made a comment under his breath. He had noticed my boobs bouncing as well. It felt really uncomfortable.

My whole body flushed with red because I was so embarrassed from the humiliation.

A few months passed and I was at a family gathering in my grandma's apartment. We would gather with extended family members from both sides of my parents' families.

I still didn't have a bra.

My grandfather had already passed away and one of his sisters was there. She happened to work for a bra company. My parents were now very much aware that I needed a bra. They evidently decided that the best time for them to talk to my great aunt about how to fit me for a bra, was in front of the entire family.

Are you familiar with the movie Sixteen Candles, where the girl gets felt up by her grandma? I got felt up by my great aunt. After grabbing my boobs in both of her hands she said, "Oh, you just need to take her to get a training bra!" And this and that. Looking back, I'm pretty sure I was well beyond needing a training bra at that point. So how embarrassing is that to get groped and talked about in front of family in-regards to getting your first bra? I started to realize there were a lot of eyes staring at my chest.

I'm sure you recall the lifeguard story I told earlier in the book. At the end of that day, I was mortified and confused when my 2 other bosses surrounded me and started asking me questions. I can't remember for certain what either one of them had said to me. I'm pretty sure they asked me to recount what I had seen. I wasn't even sure what I had seen, but they couldn't take that chance. I was damage control.

Once again, all eyes were on me…

In high school, dressing in 'less than' with my girlfriend was fun and yet drew way more attention than we had intended. Just having big boobs alone drew more than enough attention for me.

When I was 17, I worked in an Italian ice cream shop. I was the manager, and the boys who worked there were a year-or-2-younger than me. One of the boys had been flirting with me and said, "Show me your tits." I said, "I can't show you my tits out here!" He said, "Then show them to me in the back!" While he was on break, I walked into the cooler and there he was. I had gone in there to get some frozen fruit chunks that we used for making fruit shakes. He was sitting in there on a stool; he lifted his head to look at me and said, "Show me your tits." I said, "No, someone might walk into the shop."

A younger teenage boy was challenging my authority. I kept deflecting him with excuses that made sense. The attention felt good, I definitely didn't want to get caught.

When I think back to those high school days, it seems pretty desperate. Go ahead, walk all over me. Get a closer look, go ahead, cop a feel. That became my new theme song.

Why was I trying so hard to get attention and affection? "Everybody tells me I'm wrong, to want it so badly." The song lyrics from my childhood had stuck. I wanted people to like me so much that looking back, I realize I was putting myself in harm's way...over and over again. I bared almost all of me. "I've got nothing to hide." Take what you want.

On New Year's Eve, one of my high school classmates had a house party. I wasn't friends with him exactly, but I tagged along anyway because my 2 closest friends were dating 2 of his closest friends.

I wasn't the only one not coupled up that night. A few of the boys and girls didn't have dates either. They were more outgoing than me and seemed to have no trouble fitting in.

I desperately wanted these people to look at me, to notice me.

After a few drinks, one of the boys came up to me, put his hands on my boobs, and copped a feel. Although I didn't want it, I didn't stop him. Several other boys saw what was going on and wanted in on the action too. 'OMG, THEY WANT TO INTERACT WITH ME!' Just like that, it seemed like every guy at the party had touched my boobs!

It felt kind of embarrassing and exhilarating at the same time. In my mind I was thinking if the other girls were okay with their boyfriends doing that to me, I guessed that I was okay with it too. Attention was attention. Evidently it didn't matter much to me where it came from.

If I could send my younger self a message, it would be: "Hey, this isn't the kind of attention you want or deserve. You don't need to try so hard to fit in. The right people will like you for you, not for your body."

I only wish I hadn't tried so hard to get noticed.

In a twisted sort of way, I thought that this was the way to get my power back.

A healthier step in getting back my power was when I was in college. My friend and I were sitting at a bar having a few drinks. I never got drunk, because I never allowed myself to fully lose control. I always needed to be in control. Especially if I was out in a group. I wanted to make sure that my friends were always okay. I never let myself get beyond a tipsy buzzed feeling.

I tend to be a hyper aware person.

My girlfriend and I had just ordered another cranberry vodka when a guy we didn't know stepped up to the bar. He started hitting on my friend. When the bartender asked him if he wanted a drink, he sat down and asked if he could buy us a drink. We agreed and cancelled our order. Continuing our girl talk, we weren't paying much attention to what he was doing while we waited.

All of a sudden, he slid a drink our way. Thinking he was supposedly going to buy us both a drink, we just looked at each other, and then without hesitation, decided to share it. My friend and I each took a sip and almost immediately knew that something was different. It didn't taste like the drinks that we had previously been drinking.

Our mouths started to get tingly, it felt really weird. "This isn't right!" I said, and my friend agreed. Then our cheeks began to tingle. Our immediate reaction was that we needed to get this out of mouths, we needed that feeling to go away.

Looking around and not seeing any napkins, we clung tightly to one another and headed towards the restrooms. As soon as we walked through the door, my friend said, "Here, wipe your tongue with my shirt." I did and told her to do the same with my shirt.

Why we couldn't have used our own shirt sleeves is beyond me. The tingling stopped after we had thoroughly rinsed our mouths with water.

That was how we got away from the guy at the bar. I don't even remember him being creepy or trying to follow us. I do remember telling him we'd be right back and then not going back. We just wanted to get out of that place and didn't even bother to look all over for the rest of our friends. They had come in several different cabs, and our own safety was our top priority.

Chapter 11

Who You Are is Okay

Is it okay? I questioned myself on a daily basis. Am I doing the right thing? Am I going in the right direction? Am I the person that I need to be? I also spent way too much time asking other people these questions for validation. That's where I thought I needed to source my answers. I also thought I needed to be who others wanted me to be.

I am okay with who I am, whether or not anybody else is on board with that. I now realize that there are so many people who are not going to be on board with this new Chelle. They are so used to me showing up a certain way. I was always giving of myself to help others. That made things really hard.

I wasn't living my life, I lived for work. I wanted to do something different with my life. I'm no longer here just to get a paycheck. I'm now creating work that I love so I can have a life that I love. I can live my life the way that I want to and do the work that I want to do, even if other people don't get it.

It's not a work-life balance, because they're both. They are the same. I'm working for myself now. I'm not answering to somebody else and helping them grow their business. I'm also growing personally, it's not just for the other person anymore. It's me as well. It's my time.

I'm creating a business around my life. When I get more clients or things get busier, I know what I value and what I enjoy. I can base my decisions on what I feel like doing in any given moment. I have the freedom to tap into me and into the lifestyle I am choosing to create, like how relaxed I'd like to be and how much sleep I feel my body needs.

Whatever is happening in my life, my business is growing at the same time.

I now enjoy living with less pressure in my life.

Boundaries Are Important

Professional and personal boundaries are important. Boundaries certainly extend way beyond the workplace. I believe that our work environment needs to be more understanding of the little things that make a huge difference in our personal lives. Those little things that keep us afloat. For me, really understanding boundaries started right out of college when I worked as a graphic designer. I'll always be a creative, so I don't just consider myself a graphic designer. As I mentioned earlier it took about 6 months for me to find something, and 13 years later I was still at that job.

There were a lot of things that happened during those 13 years that shifted my entire mindset from being this young, naive, positive, young woman to being negative and being sick all the time. I didn't have any boundaries in the workplace or outside of the workplace to make myself feel better. I didn't even know what they would look like if I did.

My whole journey so far has been about finding self-love and self-care and putting boundaries in place so that I don't feel shitty all day long. My purpose came as part of my healing. I realized that I never wanted anyone to feel even a fraction the way I was feeling - completely burnt out. I recognized what was happening to me, but I felt powerless to stop it. So now it's my mission to empower others, so they can thrive in jobs they love, doing what they love, feeling appreciated as they step into their power.

When proper healthy boundaries start to form, and we can uphold them and say no to things, that's what creates true and lasting happiness. Having healthy detachment from our emotions, keeps us from being controlled by our emotions. If I want to take a nap right now, nothing is stopping me from taking a nap. If that's what I feel I need to be doing, I'm gonna do it.

Rather than feeling guilty, I know I will be way more productive after that nap. Why sit at my desk for 2 hours when a 10-minute cat nap will allow me to be done in 30 minutes?

Chapter 12

Your Way, Not Theirs

You don't have to be what they want you to be. It's really eye-opening to experience things in a way that you didn't know was allowed. Giving myself that permission, instead of seeking the permission from somebody else, has been very empowering. We all have that power to give ourselves permission to do the thing that makes us happy.

Compulsions

I'm definitely one of those Inbox Zero people. I hate having unread emails. It drives me nuts when I see that some people have thousands and thousands of emails that they just never get to or delete. Once I started treating this mindset as a compulsion, I was able to quickly sort through my email: 'This is crap, it's going in the trash. Alright, I need to get back to this. I'll read this later.' It used to drive me crazy to have unread emails. When I was able to step away from that compulsion, even a little bit, it cleared my mind.

I no longer needed to pour my energy into my Inbox. This allowed me the freedom to focus on doing other things.

I mentioned earlier that I had been told I would never be a success without certain people in my life and that I would never make it in becoming an entrepreneur. My boss said, "You're just going to come crawling back."

I was supposedly going to come crawling back and not do great things.

The additional thought was that what I had done for 13 years was all I was capable of doing and I could only do it with that particular boss.

Eff that.

Ultimatums

I really don't like ultimatums. If somebody tells me this is what's going to happen 'if you do this or don't do that' it's like I have a compulsion to do the opposite. That's what keeps me going, that's a challenge right there. You just told me I'm going to fail without you.

Really?

I haven't fully hit the Go button yet. You haven't even seen the real me.

So, you think this is me showing up here at two hundred percent? Let's see who comes crawling back to who.

I'm going to make it my point and my mission to not fail and to prove you wrong!

If you ask my friends, family, and coworkers about my traits they will say things like 'she doesn't give up. She keeps going. Chelle follows through and does what she says she's going to do'. All of that still remains true. The real problem for me was that I did it to a fault. Now I'm pouring those traits into a pattern of success and using them to move myself forward in my business and my life.

Trusting People

My boyfriend tells me this all the time, "not everybody's going to be your friend, not everybody is going to have your back the way that you would show up for them. You might need to take a step back and be more mindful of what's going on."

I trust people to a fault and until they give me a reason not to trust them, I'm just going to give them the benefit of the doubt. I'm going to hold space that they have my best interest as well as their own at heart. It's been a rough lesson to learn time and time again. I kick my own ass for the fact that I still stay naive and trust people as much as I do. Trusting people keeps me hopeful that there are people who are going to want to level up with me.

There are those times when I'm hesitant to trust someone. There are these little red flags along the way. When I let those red flags slide, that's when I get into trouble.

If I let things continue until something really hits, then I'm like, 'oh baby, they've been doing this the whole time. You chose to ignore it'. It's a tough balance between being naive and keeping my guard up.

Finding friends was really hard, although I've always had a lot of acquaintances. When I thought certain people were my friend and they weren't, I learned an important lesson the hard way... that some people really didn't have my back.

Chapter 13

Persevere Against All Odds

You can turn a negative into a positive. I'm living proof of that one. There's nothing wrong with perseverance. You just don't need to persevere with something that is dragging you down.

Sometimes people are very quick to tell you the thing that you need to do and yet you're still closed off to that idea. It takes time to come to that conclusion for yourself. We might have the answer in front of us, but we haven't come to that place of weighing the pros and cons in our mind. We might need to write it all out on paper and come to the full embodiment and realization that 'okay, they're right and this really is what I need to do'.

True knowledge is a thing. It's about knowing what needs to happen, not just because someone is telling me what to do. Who wants to just be a body that goes along with what everyone else is telling them? I needed to come to the realization that this was the right move for me.

Sisterhood

I believe that it's important to have at least one other person you can talk to about anything without judgment, without being worried about their reaction. Someone who is interested in having an open dialogue with you. I'm connected to a circle of awesome women, that empower each other without any worry that there's going to be any backstabbing or competition between everyone.

I'm on a mission to get women to open up. If I'm not that person that you want to open up to I totally understand. I'm not everybody's cup of tea. Find somebody who is.

I empower other women to take a leap of faith and find something that they are passionate about. It's such a great feeling. I enjoy challenging other women to do something that makes them feel good about themselves.

It's super powerful when you can finally realize that quitting doesn't necessarily mean that you failed at something. Quitting just means you're moving on to the next thing.

The Importance of Loving Yourself

It takes courage and confidence to build up love for yourself. If you don't love yourself, even though other people love you, it's impossible to feel that love.

Never Give Up

I didn't come this far to only come this far. I now want to help people by teaching them preventative measures. The things to stay away from and say no to. I want to teach them about my downfalls and how I was feeling, so that they can avoid the stress and worry that leads to a breakdown.

That's really my biggest motivation for what I do and why I want to reach young women. I'm all about teaching them to work smarter not harder, to have a voice and use it. To speak up immediately when threatened with any sexual misconduct at work.

I have a therapist and going to therapy is one of the best things I did for myself after leaving my job. I highly recommend doing that earlier. I needed an outlet to get things out in a safe place. I do want that for other women as well, whether or not I'm that person that they talk with about things.

I think everyone should have a therapist at least once in their life to be able to get things off their chest. I also understand the need for a coach to shorten your learning curve and teach you things you might not be aware of. Why wait for hindsight? We can learn from all of our mistakes and fail forward or we can learn from other people's mistakes and move forward faster.

At one point I felt so low that my parents later mentioned that they had been worried about me. They even said they were afraid that I was going to do something to hurt myself.

My response to them was "You didn't even ask, it probably scared you to ask me because you were afraid of what my response might have been." Being super independent, I allowed myself to get to the lowest of lows.

I wasn't at the point where I was going to do something to hurt myself, I just didn't know what it would look like to get out of what I was in.

I felt like Humpty Dumpty and I had to put myself back together after I fell off the wall.

Loving Yourself Isn't Selfish

Freedom-Finding Activities

Loving Yourself Isn't Selfish

What does freedom look like for you?

What does freedom feel like for you?

Have you ever felt uncomfortable at work?

Who made you feel uncomfortable?

What made you feel uncomfortable?

Do you ever feel like you have so much to do that you are letting people down?

Does the fear of letting others down keep you feeling stuck?

What would you like to change in your life?

What are your responsibilities?

Personal   *Professional/Community*

Look at your lists and circle the responsibilities you'd like to take off your plate.

Prioritize the top 10 responsibilities (you circled) that you'd like to take off your plate.

1.

2.

3.

4.

5.

6.

7.

8.

9.

10.

What are some of the things that make delegating difficult for you?

Identify some of the obstacles that get in the way...

Brainstorm some ideas to get around those obstacles...

Loving Yourself Isn't Selfish

Action Plan

Loving Yourself Isn't Selfish

List the first 3 responsibilities you'd like to delegate...

1.

2.

3.

Write out how you would delegate each responsibility...

1. Responsibility:

How I will delegate this responsibility:

2. Responsibility:

How I will delegate this responsibility:

3. Responsibility:

How I will delegate this responsibility:

Loving Yourself Isn't Selfish

About the Author

This past year has really been about transformation... with me unleashing my voice and leaving a job after 13 years. I was in a very toxic environment and I wasn't going anywhere but down. I was burnt out and sick, both physically and mentally. I didn't have any boundaries in place or know what they even looked like. I didn't stand up for myself, take care of myself or do anything to get me out of that situation. At the end of the day, it was just me.

No one was there for me. No one had my best interests in mind. They only cared that I kept getting things done for them.

When I finally had the courage to leave, it was a very defining moment of releasing my deeply rooted feelings of 'people pleasing and silencing myself'. Once I turned that corner for myself, I wanted so many people to know how to do that for themselves.

If only someone would have taken me by the shoulders early on and said "Girl! What are you doing? You need to get out of this NOW!" I didn't have that and that's why I support other young women who are looking for clarity, and a way to implement their boundaries.

My book title "Loving Yourself Isn't Selfish" brings up so many 'ah-ha thoughts' for me. For example, I don't have to 'do for other people' in order to find my happiness. I can do things for myself. It's okay to do things for myself, and it's okay to take a break. It's also okay to say no to other people. It's not a selfish thing.

In fact, it's perfectly okay to be SELFISH for yourself. I look forward to hearing from you.

You can reach me at:

www.getshelled.com or by emailing me at chelle.d@getshelled.com

On Instagram: @chellestation

My full name is Michelle. Chelle for short. I love to play with words.

The word shell represents me quite well. When I think about a shell, I think about turtle shells, seashells, and the shells baby birds come from. A shell is very structured and protective.

That's me! I am definitely a shell through and through.

Made in the USA
Middletown, DE
08 February 2021